THE
ANGLO-SAXONS

Roger Coote

Wayland

Look into the Past

Series editor: Joanna Housley
Series designer: David West
Book designer: Joyce Chester

First published in 1993 by Wayland (Publishers) Limited,
61 Western Road, Hove, East Sussex, BN3 1JD, England

British Library Cataloguing in Publication Data
Coote, Roger
    Anglo-Saxons.–(Look into the Past Series)
    I. Title   II. Series
    942.01

ISBN 0 7502 0819 8

Typeset by Dorchester Typesetting Group Ltd., Dorset,
England.
Printed and bound in Italy by L.E.G.O. S.p.A., Vicenza,
Italy.

Picture acknowledgements
The publishers wish to thank the following for providing the
photographs for this book: Lesley & Roy Adkins Picture
Library 9 (top), 15; Ancient Art and Architecture Collection
7 (both), 13, 20 (top), 23 (top), 27 (top); Bodleian Library,
Oxford 14 (bottom); British Library 11 (both), 12 (both),
16, 29 (bottom); reproduced by courtesy of the Trustees of
the British Museum 17 (bottom); C M Dixon 21 (top), 23
(bottom), 24 (bottom), 25 (bottom), 26; E T Archive 5 (top),
10, 14 (top); Robert Harding Picture Library 5 (bottom), 8,
18, 19, 22; Michael Holford 24 (top), 25 (top), 27 (bottom);
Hulton Deutsch Collection 17 (top); Syndication
International 28, 29 (top).
Artwork by Peter Bull 4; Jenny Hughes 6; Stephen Wheele 9.

CONTENTS

Words that appear in **_bold italic_** in the text are explained in the glossary on page 30.

WHO WERE THE ANGLO-SAXONS?

The Anglo-Saxons were people who came from many different tribes in northern Germany and Denmark to settle in Britain. The first Anglo-Saxons came as traders, or as soldiers in the Roman army. When the Romans left Britain in AD 410, more and more Anglo-Saxons came to settle in the country. At first they lived in areas that were not being used by the people who lived in Britain – called the Britons. Later, they began to conquer the Britons and take their land.

Northumbria

Mercia

East Anglia

Wessex

Kent

KEY

Areas of Britain the settlers occupied

Saxons

Angles

Jutes

This map shows the routes taken by the Anglo-Saxons who invaded and settled in Britain. They came from tribes of Jutes, Angles and Saxons, and they are usually known simply as Anglo-Saxons. They settled first along the east and south coasts and then moved inland. As they spread out, they either took over the native Britons or pushed them further and further west, into Cornwall, Wales and north-west England.

When the Anglo-Saxons spread inland, they forced the Britons to move west. Sometimes the Anglo-Saxons and the Britons agreed on borders between their lands. But other times the Anglo-Saxons simply decided where they wanted the border to be and then built tall earth banks and ditches to mark it. This is Offa's Dike, which was built along the border between Mercia (an Anglo-Saxon kingdom) and Wales (which was occupied by the Britons). In some places the earth bank is 4 metres high. Offa was a powerful king of Mercia, and he ordered the dike to be built in the late eighth century. ▼

▲ There is a book called the *Anglo-Saxon Chronicle*, which tells us a lot about how and when the Anglo-Saxons arrived in Britain. It was written after their invasion as a record of events and updated regularly, like a diary. This is a page from the beautifully written *Chronicle*.

CHIEFTAIN, CHURL AND SLAVE

Most Anglo-Saxons lived in small settlements. Each settlement had its own lord, and a group of settlements was ruled by a local chieftain or king. At first, England had a great many small kingdoms. As time went on, some kingdoms became more powerful and took over the lands of neighbouring kings. Eventually, there were just seven kingdoms, each with its own king.

These are the seven kingdoms that made up Saxon England. The kingdoms often fought each other and their borders did not stay the same for long. Sometimes the king of the strongest kingdom was recognized by the other kings as their overlord. In the sixth century Kent was the richest and most powerful kingdom. Northumbria became the strongest in the seventh century, and Mercia took over in the eighth century.

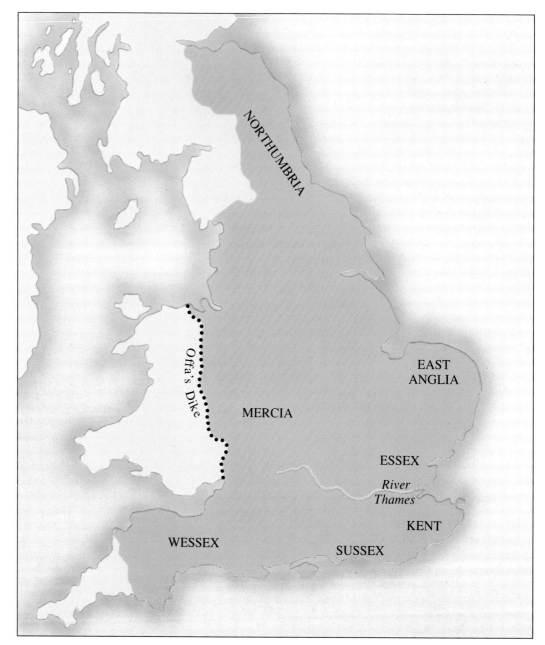

NORTHUMBRIA

Offa's Dike

MERCIA

EAST ANGLIA

ESSEX

River Thames

KENT

WESSEX

SUSSEX

During the ninth century, Wessex became the most powerful Anglo-Saxon kingdom. The statue in this picture is of King Alfred, who came to the throne of Wessex in 871 and ruled for twenty-eight years. This was a difficult time for the Anglo-Saxons, because their kingdoms were being attacked by people from Scandinavia – the Danes, or Vikings. ▶

The Danes conquered Northumbria, East Anglia and parts of Mercia and then threatened to overrun Wessex. But Alfred beat the Danes in battle and won back lands they had conquered. In 878 Alfred made peace with the Danes and agreed to share England with them.

▲ Apart from the king, the people of Anglo-Saxon England were divided into two main groups. There were freemen, who were able to own land and could travel around where they wished, and slaves, who belonged to the freemen and had almost no freedom at all. The wealthiest freemen were the king's noblemen, who were called earls or thanes. Most Anglo-Saxons were less wealthy freemen known as churls. Slaves belonged to their master and could not leave unless the master sold them or decided to give them their freedom. In this picture, a slave is holding a horse steady so that his master's wife can climb into the saddle.

AN ANGLO-SAXON VILLAGE

The Anglo-Saxon settlers avoided the towns and villas left by the Romans. Instead, they built their own villages. Each village consisted of one or more groups of small huts. Each group of huts belonged to a family, which included parents, grandparents, children, aunts, uncles and slaves. Some huts were for sleeping in and others were workshops or storehouses. At the centre of each group of huts was a large hall, where the whole family met to eat and talk.

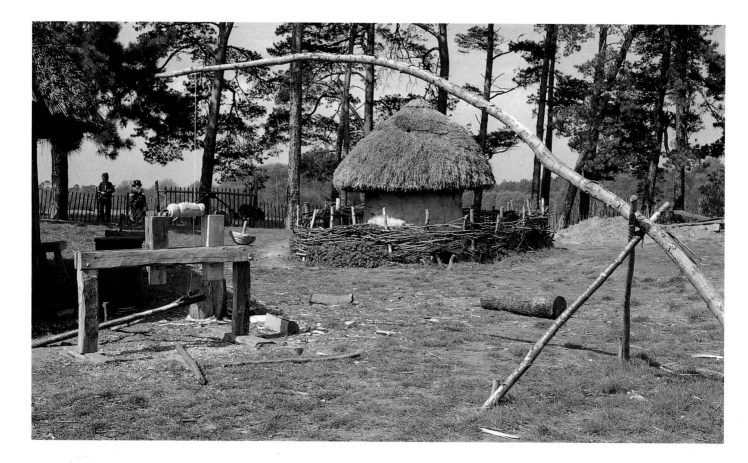

Anglo-Saxons did not build their houses from stone or brick. They used timber to construct the strong frame of a hut. Then wooden planks were nailed to the frame to make the walls. Another way of making walls was to weave thin sticks, or wattles, into panels and daub them with a layer of mud mixed with straw to keep out draughts and rain. The roofs of the huts were thatched with straw or reeds. This hut and the hut at the top of page 9 have been built to look like real Anglo-Saxon huts. They are in a village called West Stow, in Suffolk. **Archaeologists** have found the remains of an Anglo-Saxon village there.

▼ This illustration shows how a small Anglo-Saxon village might have looked. In the centre is the hall and it is surrounded by dwelling huts and workshops. The village is close to a river so that the people have a good supply of fresh water. The land on which the village was built was once forest, but the villagers cut down the trees and used the timber to build their huts. Wood was also needed to make fences and to use as fuel for heating and cooking. More forest was cut down or burned to make farmland around the village. The land was shared out among the villagers and used for growing food.

FARMING

Most Anglo-Saxons worked on the land, growing crops and raising *livestock*. The land around a village was divided into long, thin strips, which were about 1,300 to 2,000 square metres in size. The strips were shared out among the villagers, with each farmer having some strips of good, *fertile* land and some poorer land. The strips were then farmed by the 'rotation' system, in which a different crop was grown on each strip every year. For example, in the first year oats might be grown on one strip. Barley might take its place in the second year. In the third year the strip would be left fallow – *ploughed* but not planted – giving the soil a chance to regain its goodness for the next year's crop.

The lives of the Anglo-Saxons were ruled by the calendar. Most people worked on the land and had to do certain jobs at certain times of the year. In the autumn and winter, land was ploughed to prepare for sowing new crops. This plough is being pulled by four oxen. Oxen were very expensive to buy, and they were probably shared by the villagers. Anglo-Saxon ploughs were heavy and difficult to turn around at the end of a row. The fields were long and thin so that the plough did not have to be turned too often. The boy on the left is prodding the oxen with a sharp stick to keep them moving. The man behind the ploughman is sowing seeds – probably for a cereal crop, such as oats, barley, wheat or rye.

▲ Other crops were grown besides cereals, including vegetables such as peas, beans and lentils, flax for making linen, and woad and madder (plants to make dyes for colouring cloth). Most of these were planted during the spring. After the soil had been ploughed, there might still be some large lumps of earth to be broken up. In the picture above, the two men on the left are using a spade and a pick to break up the soil, while the man on the right is scattering seeds.

▼ Cereal crops were harvested during the late summer and early autumn. The stalks were cut with curved blades called sickles and the crop was loaded on to carts. Farm animals were allowed into the fields to eat the stubble that was left in the ground after harvesting. The next job was threshing – separating the cereal grains from the husks and stalks. The men in the centre of this picture are using tools called **flails** to **thresh** a crop. When the grains had been separated, they could be ground up to make flour.

▲ Anglo-Saxon villagers kept farm animals to provide food and clothing. Cattle and sheep were raised for their meat, milk and bone. The skin of cattle was used to make leather, and sheep's wool was spun and woven into cloth. Poultry was kept for eggs and meat. Most animals were kept inside during the winter, but at other times of the year they stayed outside. Pigs were usually allowed to roam in the forests and find their own food. The pigs in the picture above are eating acorns that have fallen from oak trees.

▼ Livestock were killed during the autumn to provide meat during the winter months. The meat was put in barrels and covered with salt to prevent it from going bad. As we can see in the picture below, animals were killed in a very basic way – one man is holding a goat by the horns to keep it still while the other chops off its head with an axe.

OTHER WORK

Not all the people in an Anglo-Saxon village would have worked on the land all year round. At the busiest times of the farming year, especially when crops had to be harvested, almost everyone lent a hand. But at other times some people did different jobs. For example, hunters, fowlers and fishermen caught wild animals, birds and fish for food; blacksmiths made weapons and tools from iron; and potters made clay pots for cooking and storing food.

The man in the picture is a fowler. He is using a hawk to catch birds. A fowler captured young hawks each spring and trained them to catch smaller birds with their claws and bring them back to him. Then, in autumn, the fowler set his hawks free so that he did not have to feed them through the winter. The fowler also had other ways of catching birds. He used *snares*, traps, nets or a sticky mixture called birdlime, made from plants. The fowler smeared birdlime on tree branches and twigs so that small birds would stick to it when they landed.

Every Anglo-Saxon settlement probably had at least one blacksmith. Smiths were responsible for making a huge variety of iron items. These included swords, knives, spearheads, axeheads, sickles, belt buckles, brooches, locks and keys, bowls, buckets, cups and spoons. Clearly, the blacksmith had to be very skilled to be able to make so many different things, and he would have been a very important person in the village.

14

This picture shows a replica of an Anglo-Saxon weaving **loom**. Both wool and flax were woven into cloth, although wool was more important. As well as making cloth for themselves, Anglo-Saxons also exported cloth to other countries. It may be that all girls were taught how to weave when they were young and that most clothes were made in the home. Archaeologists have found that some settlements were weaving-villages, perhaps making cloth for trade. In these villages, there were a number of buildings that were used as weaving sheds and others in which the wool and finished cloth were stored.

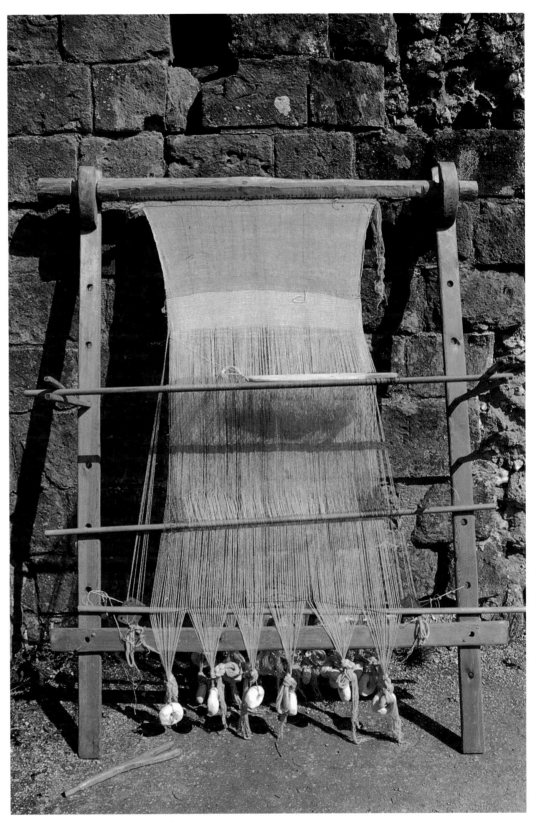

FOOD

By modern standards, Anglo-Saxon meals were probably not very exciting to eat. People ate what they could grow in their own fields or catch for themselves. Most everyday food was boiled or stewed in *cauldrons* hung over a fire. The usual dish was pottage – a cross between a soup and a stew – which was served with thick slabs of bread. Meat was a luxury and was often eaten only at feasts.

On special days throughout the year, feasts were held in the halls in Anglo-Saxon settlements. In farming villages there would be a feast to celebrate the harvest. Much grander feasts were held in a king's hall, and the nobles would swear their loyalty to their lord and would promise to risk death for him. This picture shows a feast being held in the hall of a wealthy noble. The guests are being served by slaves. They are using knives to eat their food; each guest took his or her own knife to a feast. There was usually a lot of drinking at feasts, with ale and *mead* (made from honey) being the most popular drinks.

These two boys are ▶ cooking chickens and a piglet at a feast. The boy on the right was called a 'turnspit', and his job was to turn the long iron bar so that the meat cooked evenly on all sides. The boy on the left is putting logs on to the fire. The Anglo-Saxons ate lots of different types of meat, including beef, mutton, pork and chicken, which they raised on their land, and hare, wild boar and *venison* from *game* animals caught by hunters. Most game was eaten by wealthy people, because they were the only ones who could afford to have their own hunters or had enough spare time to go hunting themselves.

▼ Pottery mugs were normally used for drinking from, but at their feasts, many Anglo-Saxons used hollowed-out animal horns. The main drawback was that if the horn was put down the liquid inside spilled out. Gradually, craftsmen became skilled at making glassware, and were able to make beautiful drinking glasses, jugs and bowls. These items would have been very expensive and were only for the wealthiest people.

CLOTHES AND JEWELLERY

Anglo-Saxon clothes were made from natural materials that could be obtained by farming and hunting. Wool from sheep and linen from the flax plant were the most commonly used fabrics. Nearly all people wore much the same type of clothes, which were well suited to farm work. Even rich people wore quite simple clothes, although the fabrics may have been of better quality. Children were thought of as small adults so they dressed in the same way as their parents.

◀ This picture shows people at a **reconstructed** Anglo-Saxon village at West Stow, in Suffolk. The men are wearing tunics which come down to just above the knee. Underneath, they have thin trousers, or leggings. Some people wore shoes made of leather (from animal skins), although others simply wrapped their feet in pieces of woollen material which they tied around their ankles. When the weather was very cold, men and boys wore long cloaks and caps.

▲ These people are pretending to be at a feast in an Anglo-Saxon hall. The women in the foreground are wearing tunics rather like those of the men, although they are much longer. The garment with a hood was called a mantle and was worn over a tunic. In cold weather, a second tunic was put on over the mantle. Most women wore their hair long.

19

The main difference between the clothes of rich people and those of the poor was the jewellery and ornaments that they wore. Most people wore some form of jewellery, but the rich could afford more expensive items. Brooches and clasps were often worn to hold garments together – zips and poppers had not been invented. Buckles were also worn on straps and belts. These two pictures show the difference in quality of Anglo-Saxon jewellery.

▲ The large, highly decorated gold buckle was found in the grave of a Saxon king, possibly Redwald, who died in 624. He was buried at a place called Sutton Hoo in Suffolk.

◀ The other buckles were found by archaeologists digging at a Saxon settlement. They are made of cheaper metals and are not so skilfully decorated.

At Sutton Hoo, ▶ archaeologists uncovered hundreds of items, including swords, spears, bowls and nails. Rich jewels were also discovered, many decorated with gold and precious stones. This is one of the king's clasps, which fastened his cloak at his shoulder.

Although the teeth of this comb have been broken off, you can see that the Anglo-Saxons used very similar objects for their hair to the ones that we use today.

21

FIGHTING AND WARFARE

Life in Anglo-Saxon England was often violent. In the early part of the Anglo-Saxon period, settlements were sometimes attacked by neighbouring chieftains, villagers were killed and livestock was stolen. The forests that lay between settlements were often home to outlaws who set upon travellers and robbed them. From the late eighth century, settlements were also attacked by fierce Viking raiders from across the North Sea. Then, in 1066, the Normans invaded from northern France, defeated the Anglo-Saxons and conquered England.

◄ When a village had to be defended against attack, the villagers would grab their weapons and fight. The most usual weapons were spears, swords and battle-axes. For protection, some men wore either a leather or *chain mail jerkin* and a helmet, and many carried a round wooden shield. The chain mail was simply put on over the top of the tunic. This man is dressed in much the same way as an Anglo-Saxon fighter might have been.

▲ This scene was carved on the side of a beautifully decorated box, which is known as the Franks casket. It was made in the early eighth century and shows a group of Saxon warriors going into battle. Some of the fighters have spears while others have swords. The spear was most often used by the ordinary men, who might have been called from the fields to defend their village. The sword was the weapon of a noble or other important person.

◀ This is the hilt, or handle, and part of the blade of a Saxon sword found in Yorkshire. It was made in the ninth or tenth century. Most of the sword is of iron, with patterned silver strips on the hilt. The Saxons treasured fine swords and sometimes gave them names. Such weapons were passed down from father to son.

The helmet and the decorations on the shield in these pictures were found in the grave at Sutton Hoo. The helmet is made of iron, decorated with other, more valuable, metals including silver. It is extremely large and was probably padded on the inside.

◀ The shield was made of wood and was almost a metre across. The wood rotted away over the centuries (the one in the picture is a modern reconstruction) leaving only the metal fittings showing a dragon, a bird of prey and other objects.

TRADE AND TRAVEL

In Anglo-Saxon times, people only travelled if they had to. Most people stayed in and around their own settlements all their lives. This was partly because most of the things they needed were made or grown nearby. Also, travelling was dangerous. Many roads passed through forests where bandits lived – people such as criminals on the run and men who had lost the protection of their master and had no way of making a living. Any traveller was a target for attack by these bandits.

◀ This purse lid was part of the treasure found at Sutton Hoo. The goods found at Sutton Hoo show that there was a great deal of trade between Anglo-Saxon England and mainland Europe: the purse lid was found with gold coins that came from France; the shield and helmet opposite were made in the Swedish style; and there were silver items from the *Byzantine Empire*.

Merchants and *pedlars* travelled around selling goods in towns and villages. People would either buy things, with coins like these, or exchange goods for other goods. ▶

RELIGION

The earliest Saxon settlers in England were *pagans* who worshipped a number of gods. The most important gods were Woden, the god of wisdom, Tiw, the god of war, Thunor, the thunder god and Frig, the goddess of fertility. The Anglo-Saxons carried out *sacrifices* to please their gods, and tried to use magic spells to get the gods to help them. When the spells were written down, letters called runes were used. In the late sixth century Christian missionaries – including Columba, from Ireland, and Augustine, from Rome – arrived in England. Gradually, they persuaded the Anglo-Saxons to abandon their pagan gods and become Christians.

The bodies of pagan Saxons were often burned and the ashes were then put in special pottery containers called urns. The urn in the picture dates from the sixth century and was found in Lincolnshire. The bodies or ashes of kings and other important Saxons were often placed in ships that were then buried under large mounds of earth. It is thought that Redwald, king of East Anglia, was buried in the famous ship burial at Sutton Hoo. By the time his burial mound was *excavated* in 1939, the wooden ship had rotted away but its shape could still be seen from marks in the soil.

Christian monks established *monasteries* ▶
where they could live and practise their faith.
The monasteries – especially those in the
north of England – became important centres
of learning and they were places where
reading and writing were taught. The monks
made beautiful copies of religious books. The
picture shows pages from the Lindisfarne
Gospels, which were made near the end of the
seventh century. They were written in Latin,
and the pages of the book were made from
flattened animal skins.

◀ As Christianity
spread, the Anglo-
Saxons converted
their pagan temples
into churches. Later,
they began building
new churches out of
stone. This one at
Bradford-on-Avon,
Wiltshire, was built
during the early
eighth century and
was added to in the
tenth century.

LEISURE AND WRITING

For most ordinary Anglo-Saxons, life was very hard and rather short – we learn from burial sites that only a small number lived to be more than forty years old. This meant that there was very little time for leisure. The main events to look forward to were probably the feasts in the hall of the village. On these occasions, there would be tastier food than usual and plenty to drink. Entertainment might be provided by travelling *minstrels*, acrobats or story-tellers.

The people in this picture are entertainers who travelled from place to place to perform at feasts and for wealthy nobles and kings. They are shown playing many different musical instruments, such as pipes, drums and a harp. Entertainers such as acrobats, jugglers and singers were often not much older than children. They might have had to leave home because their parents were too poor to look after them. Or perhaps they decided that being an entertainer was more interesting than a hard life working on the land.

28

▲ The men in this picture are using dogs to hunt a wolf. Other animals hunted by wealthy Anglo-Saxons included stags, wild boars, foxes and, perhaps, badgers. Fowling with hawks was also a favourite pastime among the rich. Such people often rode horses when they were hunting; it is thought that Saxons also used horses for racing.

This is a page from ▶ *Beowulf*, the oldest English poem. It was written between 700 and 750 (but this copy was made around 1000). The long poem is set in Denmark, and it tells the story of the hero Beowulf, who fights monsters and dragons and becomes king.

GLOSSARY

Archaeologists People who dig up and study objects from the past in order to learn about the civilizations that created them.

Byzantine Empire The eastern part of the Roman Empire, whose capital was Constantinople (now Istanbul in Turkey).

Cauldron A large pot used for cooking food.

Chain mail A type of flexible armour made from metal rings fixed together with rivets.

Excavate To dig up buried ruins.

Fertile Able to produce plenty of crops.

Flails Tools for separating grain from straw.

Game The meat from animals and birds which are hunted for sport.

Jerkin A short jacket with no sleeves or collar.

Livestock Farm animals.

Loom A machine for weaving thread into cloth.

Mead Wine made by fermenting honey.

Merchant A person who makes his or her living by buying and selling goods.

Minstrels Travelling musicians.

Monasteries Buildings where monks live.

Pagan A word used to describe any form of religion other than Christianity.

Pedlar A person who travels from place to place selling goods (usually small items).

Plough To turn over the soil of a field using a metal tool, called a plough, which is dragged through the earth.

Reconstruct To re-make a building or other object from the past by piecing together evidence of the way it looked originally.

Sacrifice To kill something in order to please a god.

Snares Traps to catch animals.

Thresh To separate grain from straw.

Venison The meat from deer.

IMPORTANT DATES

All these dates are AD

c. **410-520**   Saxons start to settle in England.

c. **563**   The Christian missionary Columba visits Iona, an island off the west coast of Scotland.

597   The Christian missionary Augustine visits England.

681   By now the whole of England is converted to Christianity. The Lindisfarne Gospel is produced.

c. **700**   The Franks Casket is made.

c. **700-750**   *Beowulf* is written, although the surviving manuscript is dated 1000.

715   Bradford-on-Avon church is built.

c. **730**   The monk, Bede, writes the *Ecclesiastical History of the English People.*

757-796   Offa is King of Mercia.

792   The Vikings raid Lindisfarne.

867   Danes conquer Northumbria and York.

871-899   Alfred is King of Wessex.

871   Danes invade East Anglia and Wessex.

954   England becomes one kingdom under the Danes.

1066   William the Conqueror leads the Norman invasion of England.

BOOKS TO READ

Saxon Invaders and Settlers by Tony D Triggs (Wayland, 1992)
A colourful book that clearly shows the Saxon influence on Britain.

Saxon Villages by Robin Place (Wayland, 1989)
This book uses illustrations to show what life was like in a Saxon village.

The Saxons by Jon Nichol (Simon & Schuster, 1990)
A book that contains photographs, original source material and questions for children to answer about the Saxons.

INDEX